WITHDRAWN
PUBLIC LIBRARY
SANTA BARBARA, CALIFORNIA

Animals with Armor
Armadillos

by Julie Murray

Dash!
LEVELED READERS
An Imprint of Abdo Zoom • abdobooks.com

Level 1 – Beginning
Short and simple sentences with familiar words or patterns for children who are beginning to understand how letters and sounds go together.

Level 2 – Emerging
Longer words and sentences with more complex language patterns for readers who are practicing common words and letter sounds.

Level 3 – Transitional
More developed language and vocabulary for readers who are becoming more independent.

THIS BOOK CONTAINS RECYCLED MATERIALS

abdobooks.com

Published by Abdo Zoom, a division of ABDO, PO Box 398166, Minneapolis, Minnesota 55439. Copyright © 2022 by Abdo Consulting Group, Inc. International copyrights reserved in all countries. No part of this book may be reproduced in any form without written permission from the publisher. Dash!™ is a trademark and logo of Abdo Zoom.

Printed in the United States of America, North Mankato, Minnesota.
102021
012022

Photo Credits: iStock, Minden Pictures, Shutterstock
Production Contributors: Kenny Abdo, Jennie Forsberg, Grace Hansen, John Hansen
Design Contributors: Candice Keimig, Neil Klinepier

Library of Congress Control Number: 2021940123

Publisher's Cataloging in Publication Data

Names: Murray, Julie, author.
Title: Armadillos / by Julie Murray
Description: Minneapolis, Minnesota : Abdo Zoom, 2022 | Series: Animals with armor | Includes online resources and index.
Identifiers: ISBN 9781098226572 (lib. bdg.) | ISBN 9781644946534 (pbk.) | ISBN 9781098227418 (ebook) | ISBN 9781098227838 (Read-to-Me ebook)
Subjects: LCSH: Armadillos--Juvenile literature. | Xenarthra--Juvenile literature. | Armored animals--Juvenile literature. | Animal defenses--Juvenile literature. | Veterinary anatomy--Juvenile literature.
Classification: DDC 599.3--dc23

Table of Contents

Armadillos 4

More Facts 22

Glossary 23

Index 24

Online Resources 24

Armadillos

Armadillos are found in Central and South America. They are also in parts of North America.

They live in grasslands and woodlands.

Armadillos have sharp claws. These help them dig.

They dig underground homes. These homes are called burrows.

An armadillo has an oval-shaped body.

The top of the head and body are covered in a hard **plate**. It is like armor.

If in danger, armadillos can lie very flat. One **species** can even roll into a ball. Their armor keeps them safe!

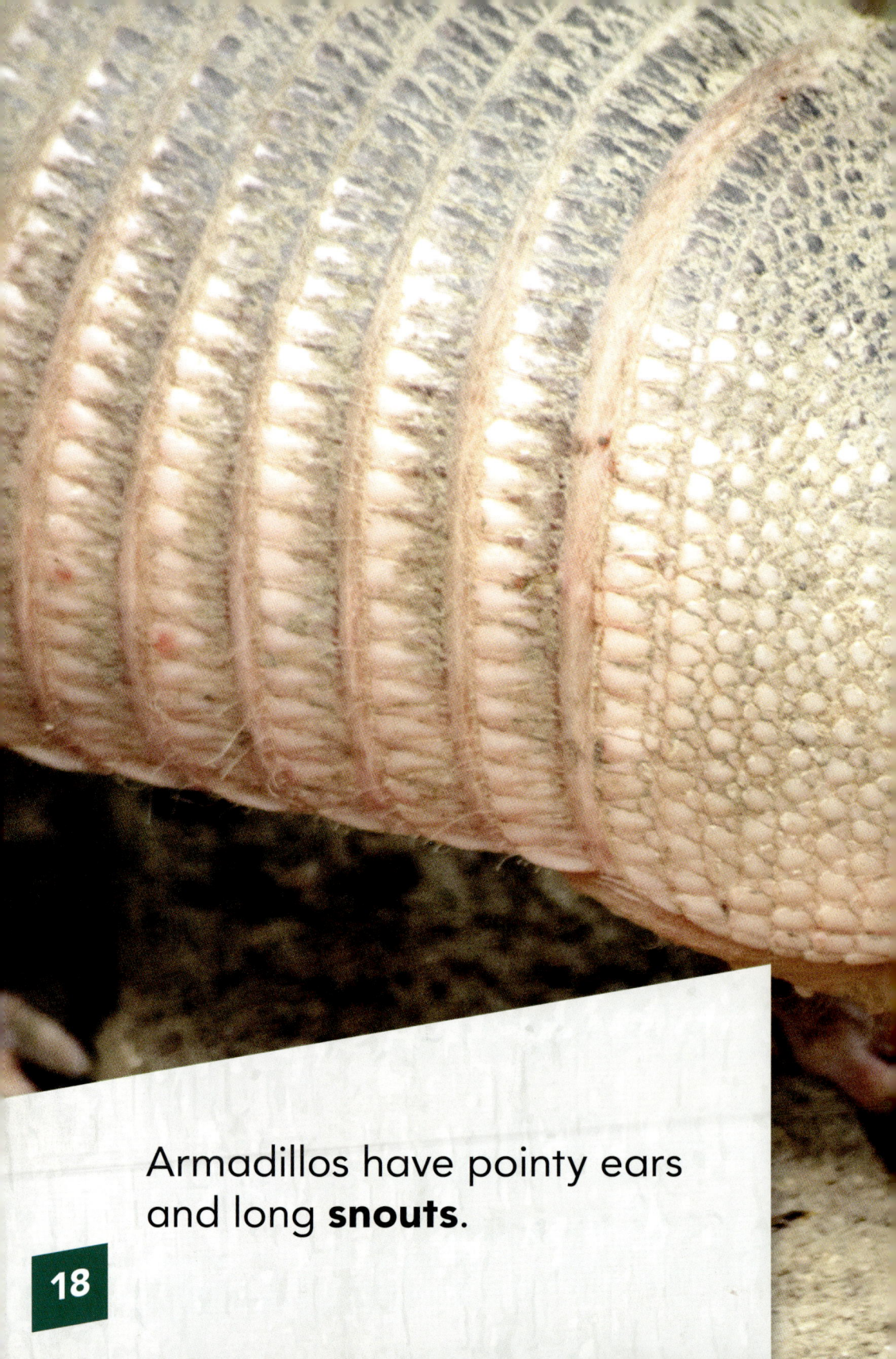

Armadillos have pointy ears and long **snouts**.

They have long, sticky tongues. Their tongues help them find and catch food.

Armadillos mainly eat insects. They also eat small animals and plants.

More Facts

- Some armadillos can jump high in the air. This scares predators away.

- Armadillos are good swimmers. They can hold their breath for six minutes underwater!

- The nine-banded armadillo is the only **species** found in the United States.

Glossary

plate – a bony covering on some animals. An armadillo's bony plates are called osteoderms. They grow in the skin.

snout – the front part of an animal's head that sticks out. The snout includes the nose, mouth, and jaws.

species – a group of living things that look alike and can have young together.

Index

body 13, 14

burrow 11

Central America 5

claws 9

digging 9, 11

food 20, 21

habitat 5, 7

North America 5

protection 16

South America 5

tongues 20

Online Resources

To learn more about armadillos, please visit **abdobooklinks.com** or scan this QR code. These links are routinely monitored and updated to provide the most current information available.